The
Collected
Satires

AMS PRESS
NEW YORK

The
Collected
Satires

of

Lord Alfred Douglas

THE FORTUNE PRESS
LONDON

Library of Congress Cataloging in Publication Data

Douglas, Alfred Bruce, Lord, 1870-1945.
  The collected satires of Lord Alfred Douglas.

  Reprint of the 1926 ed. published by the Fortune
Press, London.
  I. Title.
PR6007.086A5   1976   821'.9'12   75-41081
ISBN 0-404-14730-5

Reprinted from an original in the collections
of the University of Chicago Library
From the edition of 1926, London
First AMS edition published in 1976

Manufactured in the United States of America

AMS PRESS INC.
NEW YORK, N.Y.

DEDICATION

I DEDICATE THIS BOOK
TO THE WHOLE COMPANY OF ROSENCRANTZ AND GUILDENSTERN IN GENERAL,
AND IN PARTICULAR
TO ALL MY FALSE FRIENDS (WHOSE NAME IS LEGION),
TO ALL THOSE—MANY OF THEM BLOOD RELATIONS—
WHO, KNOWING FULL WELL THAT I WAS THE POET OF MY AGE,
AND THAT—TO QUOTE THE WRITTEN WORDS
OF ONE OF THE CHIEFEST OF THEM—
I HAD WRITTEN "BEAUTIFUL AND IMPERISHABLE THINGS",
YET LEFT ME ALONE TO FIGHT AGAINST BEASTS
WITHOUT HELP, WITHOUT COUNTENANCE,
WITHOUT SYMPATHY AND WITHOUT MONEY.
I DEDICATE THIS BOOK,
NOT TO MY INNUMERABLE ENEMIES
WHO HATED ME WITHOUT A CAUSE,
AND WHOM, BECAUSE THEY WERE MY ENEMIES,
I HAVE ALWAYS FOUND IT EASY TO FORGIVE AND TO PRAY FOR,
BUT TO THE AFORESAID FRIENDS,
WHO, WITH VERY FEW EXCEPTIONS,
HAVE SOLD AND BETRAYED ME FROM FIRST TO LAST,
BEGINNING AT WINCHESTER AND OXFORD
RIGHT DOWN TO THE PRESENT DAY.
I DEDICATE THIS BOOK
TO THE "PATRIOTIC BRITONS",

FOR WHOM, WHEN I WAS EDITING *PLAIN ENGLISH*,
I FOUGHT AND BLED AND SWEATED,
AND WHO LEFT ME IN THE LURCH
WHEN I FACED—AND OBTAINED—IMPRISONMENT
IN THE CAUSE WHICH THEY PROFESSED TO UPHOLD.
I DEDICATE THIS BOOK
TO THE "DEAR, LOVELY LADIES" OF MY YOUTH,
WHOM I REGARDED AS ANGELS OF LIGHT,
BUT WHO WERE IN TRUTH
THE COMMONEST KIND OF SELF-SEEKING WORLDLINGS
(EVEN WHEN THEY WERE NOTHING WORSE).
I DEDICATE THIS BOOK
TO THE PERSONS WHO WERE WONT TO BE SO ELOQUENT
ABOUT THE "ROTTENNESS OF THE JEWS"
AND WHO ENDED BY FORCING ME TO THINK FAR BETTER
OF THE AVERAGE JEW THAN THE AVERAGE ENGLISHMAN.
AS ALL THOSE TO WHOM I HAVE DEDICATED THIS BOOK
ARE MY FRIENDS,
I HAVE OMITTED TO PUT THEM IN THE PILLORY OF THESE SATIRES,
WHICH IS RESERVED FOR MY ENEMIES.
BUT PRIVATELY—AND METAPHORICALLY—I CONSIGN THEM ALL
TO "THE EXCELLENT WHITE BOSOM" OF JUDAS ISCARIOT,
IN WHICH PLACE (OR STATE),
SINCE THEY ARE NOT NAMED IN THESE SATIRES,
THERE IS NOTHING TO PREVENT THEM
FROM MEETING AND FRATERNISING,
AND RELIEVING THEIR CONSCIENCES *(MORE ANGLICANO)*
BY SLOBBERING OVER MY MEMORY AFTER I AM DEAD.

Preface

The late Lord Bryce, in a speech he made a few years ago, lamented the decay of satire. In fact he committed himself to the statement that in England it was a lost art. I remember reading his remarks at the time and hesitating as to whether or not it would be worth my while to write to him and point out that I had written several satirical poems and that I made bold to say that I had no more lost the art of writing satire than I had lost the art of writing poetry on the lines and in the succession of the great poets.

On reflection I came to the conclusion that it was not worth while to write to Lord Bryce, for I considered that, if my satire had anything vital in it, it could not be lost, but would inevitably crop up again sooner or later, if only after my death.

The lyrical poetry I wrote thirty years ago has been reprinted again and again, and the aggregate sale it has reached now runs into a good many thousands of copies of various books. The same applies in a less degree to my comic or "nonsense" rhymes. I mean that they have lately been reprinted after being long out of print and continue to be "good sellers". I take leave to think that this circumstance proves that my poetry is certain to live after I am dead, whatever may be the fate of ninety nine out of a hundred of my contemporaries.

Lord Bryce thought that satire was a lost art, simply because it is a fact that no leading poet except myself has written satire since Swinburne, and because the satire I have written has invariably been ignored and boycotted by the Press, which, reflecting the feebleness of this degenerate age, looks upon satire with ignorant fear and dislike.

I have just looked up, and I here record, what is the dictionary definition of the word *satire*. I quote from Chambers's admirable dictionary. " Satire—A literary composition originally in verse, essentially

a criticism of man and his works, whom it holds up
to ridicule or scorn—its chief instruments, irony,
sarcasm, invective, wit and humour : an invective
poem ".

It is quite obvious, then, that satire cannot be
polite or pleasant writing. If satire is to exist at
all, it must be savage, fierce, bitter and, perhaps
also, even occasionally unfair. I take it that a poet
writing a satire is very much in the privileged position of an advocate attacking a man in a law court,
in his opening speech. The difference is that, whereas
the lawyer speaks from his brief " on instructions ",
the poet speaks from his heart and his soul.

There may be a complete answer to the lawyer's
opening attack. Subsequent events, the evidence
which comes out in the course of the hearing of the
case, the answers given under cross-examination by
the person attacked, or admissions made by the other
side, may each and all go to invalidate the force of
counsel's original attack. Nevertheless it remains on
record. The bitterest, most virulent and scurrilous
of these satires of mine is that directed against that
"distinguished lawyer and politician ", Lord Birkenhead.
Anyone who takes the trouble to read it will see
that it was drawn out of me by way of a reply to
a very bitter, malicious and unfair attack made on

me by this brilliant advocate in a case in which I was accused of a criminal offence, that of '' conspiring '' with another person (the late T. W. H. Crosland to wit) to bring a ''false charge'' against a third person. The case was tried at the Old Bailey in my absence abroad, and, in the result, Crosland was acquitted after a trial lasting eight days, and his acquittal, of course, carried mine with it. Later, I was again the object of criminal proceedings at the instigation of the same person, and again I won my case and justified to the hilt everything I had said and written against him in the public interest.

To put the whole matter in a nut-shell, it was clearly established that Crosland and I had not "conspired to bring a false charge", but had merely formulated at great risk to ourselves a perfectly true charge, which it was in the public interest to bring. Instead of being abused and blackguarded by F. E. Smith and others, we ought to have been publicly thanked and applauded by both Houses of Parliament. Nevertheless for doing what we did, Crosland and I were both attacked with the utmost and most unscrupulous virulence, nor has that attack ever been withdrawn or apologised for. It remains on record in the published reports of the case and in that sense is just as permanent as my reply in this book. My satire on F. E. Smith may be virulent and scurrilous, it may even be unfair, but it only came as an answer—the poet's answer to the lawyer—to an attack which was more virulent and scurrilous and deliberately unfair and unjust. I reprint it now, not with the slightest idea of renewing an attack on Lord Birkenhead for what he did—speaking from his brief—all those years ago, but simply because, being the work of an established poet, it is bound to be reprinted sooner or later, and can no more be wiped out and forgotten than the work of any other established poet. The same applies *mutatis mutandis* to any of the other poems in this book. We all know that Byron lived to repudiate and apologise for " English Bards and Scotch Reviewers ". He even declared that, if it had not become the property of someone else, he would have destroyed it. But this, of course, was mere talking. Byron himself could not have destroyed " English Bards and Scotch Reviewers " after he had once published it. It was out of his power, and must always have remained out of his power, to take back what he had written and what had been read by countless thousands of readers. And to this day, it remains one of the finest satires ever written. Who now bothers about its undoubted unfairness and scurrility ?

All the satires in this book have already been published and widely circulated, and I could not annul them, even if I wished to do so. I collect them now and offer them to those who are interested in satire, simply as literary objects of interest or curiosity. The passion of anger and indignation which inspired them is as dead today as are the fires that inspired the earliest love poem which I wrote when I was still a boy at Oxford. The persons who are pilloried or attacked in these satires may possibly feel aggrieved, but they are all either persons who attacked me unfairly and tried to injure and actually to ruin me, or alternatively, persons whose public conduct has, at one time or another, made them legitimate objects of satire and censure. I stress the word "public" because I for my part would never consider that I was entitled to pillory *private* vices or failings of any human being. To do so would be to violate the principles of Christian charity and to be guilty of "detraction" in the true theological sense of that word.

I stoutly deny that any poem in this book can be fairly so stigmatised. I wrote all these poems either in sheer self-defence against cruel and malignant attacks on myself, or as the result of genuine moral indignation. Persons who unfairly attack or ill-treat a man who happens to be a poet and gifted with the power of hitting back poetically, have only themselves to thank for what they get. In the long run, it is well to remember, the poet always gets the last word. Nor has there ever lived a considerable poet who did not possess the weapon of satire in his armoury. The extent to which any given poet has used that weapon depends, generally speaking, on the sort of treatment he has had from his contemporaries. Looking at my own published work in the light of that postulate, I think I can fairly say that no poet that ever lived has had more justification for the use of satire than myself and that, considering the provocation, few have used it more sparingly.

ALFRED BRUCE DOUGLAS.

October, 1926.

PROLOGUE

Prologue

Still must I hear ? Shall " Balmy Eve " make boast,
All unrebuked, to mock the choiring host ? (*)
Shall Darling pull the strings and Avory bleat,
While Justice weeps behind the judgment seat,
Because, defenceless from the felon knock,
Bound Poetry stands muzzled in the dock ?
Shall Astbury, inspired by Edmund Gosse,
Injunct the truth to shelter Robert Ross ?
Shall Bray bray on for ever while he passes
Unpilloried among his brother asses ;
While through his spectacles' distorted glint
Strabismic Strachey's Spectatorial squint

(*) " I have no ear for music and still less for poetry ". — Mr. Justice Eve
in a recent " judgment ".

Insults the Poet with envenomed glare,
And Beaverbrook and Harmsworth taint the air ?
The mills grind slow, All Fools' Day seems unending,
But at long last the Poet gets them bending.

THE RHYME
OF F DOUBLE E

The Rhyme of F Double E

Said Robert Ross to Smith : " F. E.,
The ' Movement ' is in jeopardy,
But you can pull us through I think,
If Sheeny Lewis tips the wink.
Our witnesses I'm sure you'll find
The sort congenial to your mind.
There's Charlie Garratt ; he's in jail
For offering himself for sale.
Just as you lawyers do. (How sad
To think the Law condemns a lad
For playing such a useful *rôle*
It 's too absurd upon my soul.)
Lewis has put him in the way
He knows exactly what to say.
Then there's Chris Millard, such a dear,

You *will* like him : he too, I fear,
Has done a little bit of time
For what the silly Law calls " crime "
But that won't put you off I know,
For did not our dear Oscar go
Through the same martyrdom and thus
Pre-sanctify the way for us ?
Excuse me, Mr. Smith, if here
I pause to shed a pious tear.
I know you feel, as we all do,
That what that suffering Saint went through
Remains a national disgrace ;
We heard you in the Ransome Case,
And our hearts warmed to you at once ;
If Lewis had not been a dunce,
He would have briefed you from the first
Instead of Wild ; but that's the worst
Of little Georgie. He's so rash
And *so* impulsive, full of dash
And sticks at nothing (that's his merit)
And sharp and nippy as a ferret,
But lacks his father's hard jew sense.
I begged him not to spare expense
I had the money there you see
For all the ' Movement ' 's backing me.

But Lewis *would* have Wild, he thought
No other leader could be bought
To do the dirty work, the fool
Mistrusted his own golden rule.
Would you believe he'd go so far
As quote " the honour of the Bar ? "
That ancient worn-out hoary myth,
Would you believe it, F. E. Smith ?
He did indeed; I winked and smiled,
But he was firm. Then as to Wild,
Of course the *name* appealed to me,
Even without the final " E ".
" What's in a name ? " fair Juliet sighed,
And " what's an E " George Lewis cried.
Wild without " E ", he seemed to think,
Could raise at least as great a stink,
As the real Wilde. And so I own
We took our Wild to Marylebone.
And there he played at " tug-of-war "
With Mr. Arthur Comyns Carr
Instructed by a Mr. Bell,
(Such a nice man) and all went well
Till Crosland got into the box
And handed out some dreadful knocks.
One, two ; one, two — a single bout,

And our poor Wild was " down and out ".
But you must try a different plan,
And go for Douglas, he's the man.
Wade in and make a foul attack;
He won't be there to hit you back.
Slander and lie, spit out black dung,
Vomit red venom, steep your tongue
In gall and bitterness, the Devil
Will help his own, the powers of evil
Will hover round in unseen flight
To fortify their chosen knight.
" Wilde and the Movement " be your cry,
All the dear " comrades " will stand by
To cheer you on, the Court will be
Packed with our choicest chivalry,
The fairest Gitons of the town,
With scented locks, fair, red or brown,
Curled *à la Garratt,* and rouged lips,
And powdered cheeks and rolling hips,
And sweet shrill voices, clamant with
The praises of " dear Mr. Smith ",
Will rally round your standard daily
And make a sump of the Old Bailey.
In this congenial atmosphere
Your native talents will appear,

You'll smash old Crosland, a mere boor,
A " minor author " ill and poor,
With only Hayes to help him out.
He knocked out Ernest Wild no doubt,
But you're a different pair of horses,
You'll eat him up in several courses.
A man who's not ashamed, just think,
To stand a charwoman a drink.
How low, *how* common ! You and I,
My dear F. E., would rather die
Than so degrade ourselves, but we
Are in the best society.
I'm " right in " with the Asquith set,
In fact I'm Mrs. Asquith's pet,
And one thing's certain, lose or win,
She'll stick to me through thick and thin.
You should have seen the way she backed me
When that infernal brute attacked me—
(Douglas I mean) at Queen Anne's Gate,
At the Glenconner's, why she sat
And positively held my hand
Till he went out, Oh, it was grand,
With all his people glowering round.
But thanks to her I held my ground.
And what was even more and better

She made Glenconner write a letter
Full of servile civility,
It 's been most valuable to me,
And your position is immense
Thanks to George Wyndham's influence.
How kind he was to you we know ;
It's strange that both of us should owe
Our present brilliant social stations
Chiefly to Douglas's relations
But so it is.   Dear simple folk —
And they don't see it, that's the joke.
I used to keep a little shop,
And here I am right on the top.
Your time with Dukes and Lords you spend,
You that were " Bottomley's young friend "
What luck for you he took you up,
And what a rise since then. Your cup
Is surely full, and poor old Bot
Can take a back seat now ; eh, what ?
But now to business, here's the "stuff",
Five hundred guineas.! — Not enough ?
Oh come ! I say, we'll make it six,
Or eight, don't put me in a fix.
You want a thousand ? Oh, dear Lord,
I simply won't. I can't afford...

Not a quid less ? Well you *are* hot.
You're a sheer credit to old Bot.
So be it then, coin isn't lacking,
I've got a pretty solid backing.
There's Dash and Blank and You-Know-Who,
The " hooded M. P. " Lewis, too,
Will stretch a point to help I know,
He loathes, and fears Lord Alfred so,
And Crosland, too, he hates like Sin,
He'd give his soul to " do them in ".
And while I think of it, F. E.,
I'll drop a line to Colonel C...,
He'll lend a hand to help us through ;
We are so popular, our crew.
The Movement 's spreading very fast
We'll rope the whole town in at last,
And then what glorious times we'll have,
We'll raise dear Oscar from his grave,
And build a temple to the cult
And you shall sing " Quicunque vult "
For the new Faith. And now farewell !
Long live the cult, three cheers for Hell !
Hell on Earth and the devils loose,
(Broth of Hell and stew in the juice)
Consign all prudes to shame and sorrow

And up with Sodom and Gomorrah. ”

★　★　★

Thus Robert Ross to Smith, K. C.,
Who straight agreed to earn his fee,
By making, without conscience clause,
The worse appear the better cause.
Small time he took his brief to con
But put the Sophist's mantle on,
And forth from lucre-purchased lips
Came sneers and gibes and twisted quips,
And ugly lies with fair words drest,
Spawn of the devil in his breast,
Got on low greed and lust for gold,
When Faith was dead and Honour sold.
But all in vain, for Truth is great
And shall prevail. The Syndicate
Of perjured Sodomites sat there
And gnashed their teeth and tore their hair
And all their bottle-holding crew,
Lister and Wild and George the jew,
Looked on aghast with grief and pain
(The tears of Millard fell like rain).
Never was such complete disaster,
The great F. E. had met his master !

For Crosland tore him limb from limb
And wiped the dusty floor with him.
And Cecil (*) upper-cut him sweetly,
And the Judge finished him completely.
The Court was full of grins and chuckles
When Avory rapped him on the knuckles
And took him down a score of pegs,
Till with his tail between his legs,
Like a well-walloped fox-hound pup,
He bolted at the summing-up
So much for Smith. He stands revealed :
The " gentleman " is hairy-heeled
Under his patent leather boots,
His " get-up " at the ducal " shoots "
Of Blenheim's smirking auctioneer
Is just sartorial veneer
To hide a very ugly heart
That's filled up with " exchange and mart ".
His sentiments are so much tripe
And he'll be rotten before he's ripe

(*) Mr Cecil Hayes, Crosland 's counsel ; Crosland was at first represented by Mr Comyns Carr, instructed by Messrs Carter & Bell, but changed his legal representatives after his committal for trial.

Now Freddie Smith we know you for
A tainted Privy Councillor,
A hireling who will prosecute
For any Sodomitic brute
Who thinks you worth your dirty fee, —
Bottomley's boy, the dud K. C.,
Who pawns the honour of the Bar
To pay for a new motor-car.
A mixer up of wrongs and rights
A smiler upon catamites.
A master of low-down decrying
Whom Avory J., pulled up for lying.
A " moral bankrupt " fine and large
Who cannot hope for his discharge.
Ah, Freddie, Robert Ross's kiss
Was fatal to your hopes I wis,
As gin was fatal to the parrot
Or Millard's kiss to the boy Garratt !
Who'll look at you again, dear Fred,
Lives there a man with soul so dead ?
Even in Ulster they'll eschew you,

And in " the House " askance they'll view you.
You'll hear them whisper : " We can't sit
Upon this honest floor with *IT*.
Oh, Smith, you've taken Ross's " thou ",
You'll take the Chiltern Hundreds now ! "

When I wrote this rhyme in 1914, I did not know as much about the true in-wardness of English politics as I know now, or I should not have committed myself to this rash prophecy. I was so far "out" that Lord Birkenhead may truly say that, since he put up his great fight for Robert Ross & Co., he has never " looked back ". And only two years ago, a Daniel come to judgment, he was solemnly rebuking Mr Cecil Hayes in a newspaper article for " violating the traditions of the Bar" by daring (in defence of his client and on the instructions contained in his brief) to deal straightly in cross-examination with one of our great political mandarins, who was called as a witness in a case in which he should have been the prosecutor.

THE ROSSIAD

The Rossiad

FOREWORD

The appended diary of events will assist readers of this Satire to a comprehension of the extraordinary facts with which it deals.

FEBRUARY, 1914. *Lord Alfred Douglas writes a letter to the Prime Minister containing certain accusations against Mr Robert Ross, Mr Ross being at that time Assessor of Picture Valuations to the Board of Trade, a post created for him by Mr Asquith and carrying with it a salary of £ 1,000 a year. Mr Asquith ignores this letter.*

APRIL 1914. *Mr Ross prosecutes Mr Crosland for conspiring with Lord Alfred Douglas to bring a false charge against him.*

JUNE, 1914. *Mr Crosland tried at the Old Bailey and acquitted after a trial lasting eight days before Mr Justice Avory. Mr Ross is represented by Mr F. E. Smith, who was afterwards knighted and appointed Attorney-General to the Coalition Government under Mr Asquith.*

JULY, 1914. *Lord Alfred Douglas publishes and circulates " The Rhyme of F Double E. "*

NOVEMBER, 1914 *Lord Alfred Douglas tried at the Old Bailey on criminal charge of libelling Ross. Lord Alfred Douglas pleads justification, that is to say, undertakes to prove that everything he has written about Ross is true and written in the Public Interest. Lord Alfred Douglas calls fourteen witnesses, and goes into the witness box himself and submits to cross-examination. After a trial lasting eight days before Mr Justice Coleridge, there is a disagreement of the Jury. Nine members of the Jury, including the Foreman, wait for Lord Alfred Douglas outside the Court and express to him their regret that owing to the determined refusal of one juryman to bring in a verdict against Ross, he, Lord Alfred Douglas, has been robbed of the verdict to which he was entitled. Lord Alfred Douglas instructs his solicitors, Messrs Carter & Bell, to write to the Attorney-General (then Sir John Simon) to say that he will not consent to a* nolle prosequi *but insists on his right to be tried again and to establish his Plea of Justification. Thereupon Mr Wild, K. C., representing Ross, approaches Mr Comyns Carr, representing Lord Alfred Douglas, and offers on behalf of Sir George Lewis, Ross's solicitor, to pay all Lord Alfred Douglas's taxed costs and out of pocket expenses, and to give certain undertakings if Lord Alfred Douglas will consent to allow a* nolle prosequi *to be entered.* On these terms Lord Alfred Douglas consents to a* nolle prosequi, *the Plea of Justification remaining on the file of the Court at the Old Bailey.*

DECEMBER, 1914. *The Committee of the Reform Club, of which Mr Ross is a member, decides, after discussion, NOT to expel him from the Club or request him to resign.*

JANUARY, 1915. *Lord Alfred Douglas writes to the Prime Minister reminding him of his previous letter about Ross in February, 1914, and giving full details of the result of the trial at the Old Bailey, particulars of the charges, number of witnesses, the action of the Foreman and the other Juryman, etc., etc. The following quotation from the letter, (copy of which is in the hands of Messrs Carter & Bell, Lord Alfred Douglas's solicitors), gives an indication of its tenour : —*

> " I am credibly informed that you still continue to receive Ross in your house and to allow your wife to associate with him. I am loath to believe this, however, and I write this letter partly to give you an opportunity of assuring me that it is not true, and partly to give you exact and precise information as to the result of my trial at the Old Bailey for libelling Ross by calling him a sodomite and a blackmailer. I do this in order that you may not be in a position to pretend ignorance of the matter."

This letter is ignored by Mr Asquith.

---

* A nolle prosequi, *that is, leave to abandon the prosecution. The result being that the Defendant was acquitted and discharged, and the Plea of Justification established and placed on the record of the Court where it remains in perpetuity.*

MARCH 29, 1915. *There appears in* " The Morning Post" *and other journals an account of a presentation to Mr Ross. The presentation takes the form of an address and a sum of seven hundred pounds. The address is as follows :* —

To Robert Ross.

" *We, whose names are set down below, claim to be counted among your friends, or at least your admirers. We desire in the first place to state publicly our recognition of your services to Art and Literature. You have long been distinguished for the justice and courage of your writings, and you have illuminated the expression of your views with humour and resource. Your work as a Man of Letters, however, is but a small part of the useful energy which you have shown in many directions. You have been conspicuous for the generosity with which you have put yourself at the disposal of all who claimed your sympathy or your help. You have been one of the earliest amongst us to observe new talent and one of the most zealous to encourage it.*

By these qualities you have earned what we desire to record, our esteem and regard for one who has proved a brave, loyal, and devoted friend."

The list of signatories to this extraordinary document, drawn up by Mr Edmund Gosse, includes the names of Mr and Mrs Asquith.

Among the others signatories are : —
The Earl of Plymouth, Sir Coleridge Kennard, Mr. Agg. Gardner, M. P., Mr. More Adey, Mr. Frank Hird, Mr. Bernard Shaw, Mr. and Mrs. Emil Mond, Mr. Schiff, Mr. Schiller, K. C., Miss Schuster, Sir Isidore Spielmann, Mr. Strauss, Sir George Lewis, Lady Lewis (née Marie Hirsch of Mannheim), Mr. Charles Rothenstein, Mr. Heinemann, Mr. William Rothenstein, Mr. Gutenkunst, Mr. Robert Trevelyan, Mr. Arthur Ponsonby, M. P., Mr. Phillip Morrell, M. P., Mr. G. Lowes Dickinson, Mr. J. L. Garvin, Mrs. Leverson, Mrs. Charles Hunter, Lady Ottoline Morrell, Mrs. Carew, Mrs. Allhusen, Miss Lawrence Alma Tadema, Mr. H. G. Wells, Mr. Methuen, Mr. Robert Harborough Sherard, and the Bishop of Birmingham.

Mr. Robert Ross, in accepting the testimonial and gift of money, gracefully intimates that he would like to devote the latter to a " public object." The Senate of the University of London thereupon gives evidence of " humour and resource" by accepting the money to found a SCHOLARSHIP FOR BOYS, to be called the " Robert Ross Scholarship."

The following London daily papers, to their credit, did not print the account of the

Ross testimonial and presentation: "The Standard," "The Daily Express," "The Daily Chronicle," "The Evening Standard," and "The Globe." *A full account, set out in a prominent place, with the names of a selection of the signatories, appeared in* "The Times," "The Morning Post", "The Daily Telegraph," "The Daily Mail," "The Daily News," *and* "The Westminster Gazette"; *while* "The Pall Mall Gazette," *under the editorship of Mr. J. L. Garvin, devoted half a page to the matter, and gave a complete list of the signatories, amounting to nearly three hundred names.*

Mr. Charles Palmer, of "The Globe," *alone among London editors, had the courage and sense of duty to the Public Interest, to admit into his columns a letter from Lord Alfred Douglas containing a protest against the outrage to public decency involved in the action of the Prime Minister and the other signatories. No other paper would print a letter, though many were written, and though Lord Alfred Douglas personally approached nearly every editor in London. The magnitude of the scandal was admitted on all sides, but sheer "funk" and dread of reprisals on the part of the powerful coterie involved, prevented any protest. Most of the editors approached, while admitting and deploring the scandal, pleaded that it would be " unpatriotic to attack the Prime Minister in war time." To such a pitch of ignominious and slavish subjection had eight years of " Wait-And-See" reduced what was once the most independent and public-spirited Press in the world.*

APRIL, 1915. *The action against Ross for malicious prosecution, instituted by Mr. Crosland immediately after his acquittal in June, 1914, comes on for trial before Mr. Justice Bray and a special jury in the High Court. Mr. Justice Bray refuses to allow the case to go to the jury, on alleged technical legal grounds. In the course of his speech conveying this remarkable decision, Mr. Justice Bray refers to Lord Alfred Douglas as a man who* "was not above trumping up a false charge," ("Times" report). *Messrs. Carter & Bell, on Lord Alfred Douglas's behalf, write to the learned Judge and request an explanation. Their letter is returned unanswered by the Judge's clerk.*

Lord Alfred Douglas, after vainly endeavouring to induce the editor of "The Times" *to insert a letter in reply to the outrageous attack made on him by Mr. Justice Bray in the above-quoted words, as reported in* " The Times" *and in no other newspaper, writes to* "The Globe" *a letter which appears in that journal on the 23rd April, and of which the following is a copy: —*

SIR. — *May I beg for a small space in your esteemed columns to call attention to the following remarkable facts?* " The Times" *of last Saturday, April*

17, contained a report of Mr. Justice Bray's speech in giving judgment in the case of Crosland v. Ross (malicious prosecution), which included these words : —

> *Mr. Crosland and Lord Alfred Douglas were at that time in close association, and Mr. Ross could not ignore that one of them (meaning Lord Alfred Douglas) was writing these letters, which showed that he was not above trumping up a false charge.*

Now, it has been already made perfectly clear to the readers of " The Globe" that, so far from trumping up a false charge against Mr. Ross, I deliberately made a series of definite and specific charges against him, and that when he prosecuted me for criminal libel at the Old Bailey, I pleaded justification — that is to say, I undertook to prove that every word I had written about Mr. Ross was true, and written in the public interest. The jury disagreed after a trial lasting eight days, and a nolle prosequi was entered, Messrs. Lewis & Lewis (Mr. Ross's solicitors) agreeing to pay the whole of my costs and personal expenses incurred in my defence after taxation. My Plea of Justification remains on the file of the Court at the Old Bailey, and will remain there as long as the courts continue to exist.

Whether in face of these facts it can be considered fair and right that Mr. Justice Bray should from the Bench, in a case in which I am not directly concerned, accuse me of being " not above trumping up a false charge," I leave it to your readers and to the British public to decide. — I am, Sir, your obedient servant,

ALFRED BRUCE DOUGLAS.

NOVEMBER 6, 1915. *The Coalition Government under Mr. Asquith seizes and suppresses* "The Globe."

NOVEMBER 20, 1915. *The Government allows* "The Globe" *to re-appear under new editorship, Mr. Charles Palmer being removed from the post of editor.*

Said Edmund Gosse to Robert Ross,
" You have sustained a cruel loss,
You've lost your job, you've lost your case,
But I'll contrive to save your face.
Less than a dozen years ago
A man who had been shown up so
Would have been settled once for all,
Finished, wiped out beyond recall.
The most he could have dared to hope
Would have been for sufficient rope
To give him time to get away
Across the Channel, there to stay
Away from England all his life.
But times are changed, the country's rife
With people of ' progressive views '
Nor are they ' mostly German Jews, '
As some fool said not long ago,
We've seen them, and we ought to know.
True, Germany (like classic Rome
In its decline) is now the home
To which all cultured spirits soar
In spite of this unhappy war,
And you would doubtless find a ' pal ' in
Our dear friend Haldane's friend, Herr Ballin,
But that is neither here nor there,

London's the place. How they would stare,
Those fellow-citizens of Lot's,
At some of our compatriots
Who've done their best to build again
Those grand old Cities of the Plain.
For London in the cultured sin
Can give points even to Berlin.
So cheer up, Robbie, lift your head,
You're never finished till you're dead.
Brazen it out and cut your loss
And trust your old friend, Edmund Gosse.
I've got a plan, at one fell swoop,
To whitewash you and ' make a swoop '
Such as ' the Movement ' never knew
(*Toujours l'audace,* how true, how true!)
It's great, it's noble, it's baronial,
It's this: a Public Testimonial.
It sounds impossible enough,
But nowadays the biggest bluff
Is what gets home. Sheer impudence
Will pull you through, when commonsense
Would seem to say that all is lost.
Trust me, I've reckoned up the cost.
I've sounded Margot, and she's game
To sign, and make *Him* do the same.

How's that ? 'The Premier and his Wife,'
The head and fount of social life ?
(At least, that's what the middle classes—
Our classes—think, the silly asses.)
Once I have got 'Old Squiffy' booked.
The trick is done, the fish is hooked.
Three hundred names ! you understand
That's the big fish I mean to land.
'Letters and Art' to fill the ranks,
A few Professors, and some cranks,
A Bishop, (Anglican, I fear,
I can't work miracles, my dear,)
A brace of snobbish journalists,
(Garvin for one,) some 'optimists',
Nine or ten 'cultivated' Peers,
Some gushing ladies, poor old dears,
Victims to vapours and anæmia,
And then the riff-raff of Bohemia
To swell the list and fill it out,
The Press will do the rest, no doubt.
You'll see, they'll take it 'lying down,'
There's not an editor in town
Who'll dare to raise a single whine
When Asquith bids him toe the line.
The " *Morning Post* " ? Go on, why, Gwynne

Will be the first to put it in.
Northcliffe object ? Don't be a dunce,
He 'll be ' all over it' at once,
Trust him—and so will all the rest,
They' ll be tremendously impressed.
The Public Conscience ? why, you're mad,
There isn't such a thing, my lad.
It died ten years ago, its hearse
Was paid for by the Public Purse,
A much more potent entity.
But there—just leave it all to me.
Half those who sign will be like you,
Bien pensants, men who share our view
That all this humbug about ' vice'
Is simply worn-out prejudice.
The other half won't have an inkling
What it all means, and in a twinkling
They 'll find themselves committed to
Views which would turn their faces blue
If they were realised ; but that's
Their own look-out, such feeble flats
Won 't dare complain, and half the fun
When once they find out what they've done
Will be to mark their perturbation
And agonised determination

To keep up, in their own defence,
The legend of your ' innocence.'"

* * *

Thus did our Gosse his talents spend
To raise the spirits of his friend.
Nor were his words an idle boast
As witness, in the " *Morning Post* "
The ' fashionable news ' flung down
A challenge to a gaping town,
Of how our peerless ' Wait-and-See '
The pillar of Democracy,
The pious Nonconformist's pride
And his no less illustrious bride
Graced with their names the glowing scroll
Presented to that noble soul,
That ' man of letters ' (think of it !)
That ' loyal friend ' R. Ross, to wit,

* * *

O England, in thine hour of need,
When mounted Death on his pale steed

Rides through thy ranks and with sharp scythe
Reaps of thy noblest sons his tithe,
When far beyond thy foam-washed gates
The bloody fields of alien states
Lie weltering in thy trampled blood,
While reeling in the furious flood,
Stabbed at by snakes of under-seas,
Thy galleons beat against the breeze,
Guarding thy silver-girdled shores ;
When at thy gate the mad wolf roars,
And poisoned slime from his flecked mouth
Taints all thy blossom-breathing south,
Call on thy God, cast out thy sin !
The foe without, the foe within
Are at thy throat.   Infernal powers
Bend on this votive land of ours,
This Island once the bourne of saints
Where Vice now reigns, and Virtue faints,
And cries in vain to outraged laws,
While cynic ' Justice ' twists the cause
To the fee'd side.   Go, bow the knees,
And make thy prayers thine argosies
Across the sea of Doubt and Pride
To the old Faith thou hast denied ;
Make, ere the Furies sound thy fate,

Thine agony articulate;
Raise up the best, hack down the worst,
Tear from thy heart the thing accurst.
Two foes thou hast, one there, one here,
One far, one intimately near,
Two filthy fogs blot out thy light—
The German, and the Sodomite.

January, 1916.

ALL 'S WELL
WITH ENGLAND

All 's well with England

Scorn not the " literary executor ".
He is officially condoned, for he
Has lifted Oscar Wilde from obloquy
And planted him in our hearts' inmost core.
Behold the signatories take the floor!
Plymouth and Beauchamp, Gosse and Shaw, and see
Budding around the genial Beerbohm Tree,
Schiff, Schiller, Schuster, Spielmann and some more.

Out there in Flanders all the trampled ground
Is red with English blood, our children pass
Through fire to Moloch. Who will count the cost?
Since here at home sits merry Margot, crowned
With Lesbian fillets, while with front of brass.
" Old Squiffy " hands the purse to Robert Ross.

1916.

TO A CERTAIN JUDGE

To a Certain Judge

Master of dubious arts, the sophist's cloak
Rests all too aptly on your cynic mind.
Justice we know is never quite so blind,
Under her hood-winked eyes, as simple folk
Simply suppose. A deft judicial spoke
Thrust in her wheel, a crooked push behind,
Invisibly bestowed, are, in their kind,
Cantrips that cozen, jury-fogging smoke.

England expects, when ministerial boots
Accite subservience to the lingual task,
Vigour and zeal. Your ludship's verbal grace
Outshines the varnish that your tongue salutes.
Red-robed automaton, behind your mask
You hide (too obviously) a leering face.

Wormwood Scrubs. 1924.

SHAKESPEARE'S TERCENTENARY
A MASQUE

Shakespeare's Tercentenary
A Masque

SCENE: *A vast theatre packed with people. Mr Robert Ross, Sir George Lewis and Sir F. E. Smith occupy the Royal Box. The curtain rises and reveals the Shaespeare Tercentenary Committee consisting of a few gentlemen with German-Jewish names, headed by Mr Asquith (the President) who carries a large laurel wreath, Lord Plymouth, Sir George Alexander and Mr Mackail. The Committee is grouped around a colossal* papier maché *statue of Shakespeare :*

SENNET :   *Enter Prologue, who speaks as follows :*

This is great Shakespeare's tercentenary,
And consequently lo! the German Jew
(As is most meet) supported by a few
Distinguished gentlemen.   They needs
        must be

Culled from the Ross-admiring galaxy
Who lately gave to that sweet soul his due
(Bowing to Ross)
Therefore let no dog bark and no cat mew
Before our President, great " Wait-and-
See ".
(Mr Asquith advances and bows)
George Alexander, Plymouth and Mackail
I now present, staunch " Rossites "
every one,
And lovers, too, of " that unhappy child " (*)
(To quote " F. E. ") " of genius " *(Turning
toward statue of Shakespeare)* Shakes-
peare hail !
We bring this garland. *(Mr Asquith, inter-
posing)* Wait a bit, what fun,
Let's give the wreath instead to Oscar Wilde.

*(Loud applause from the Royal Box. Mr Asquith thereupon hands the wreath
to Oscar Wilde's " literary executor ", Mr Robert Ross, who returns thanks in a
voice choked with emotion. Frantic cheers from the audience [I don't think] —
Curtain....)*

1918.

(*) " Oscar Wilde, that unhappy child of genius ", words quoted from
speech made by Sir F. E. Smith at the Ransome trial.

EVE AND THE SERPENT

Eve and the Serpent

Scene THE LAW COURTS, . . . CHANCERY DIVISION.

Enter the Devil, attired as a Judge.   He speaks:

St George for England ?   No—not in these courts,
The dragon here is much more in our line.
We take the winning side.   Someone retorts,
" St George o'ercame the dragon."   I opine
That that was in a figurative way,
Or took place in some super-sensual sphere.
The super-sensual " cuts no ice " to-day,
" The other world " does not concern us here.
We don't go in for ethical conceits,
And " abstract Justice " leaves us very cold.
In this arena of forensic feats

The most persuasive influence is gold ;
To put the thing poetically.—fees,
To put it baldly. Counsels' fees of course
Are what I mean, for all the world agrees
That Incorruption is the motive force
Of English Justice. Judges can't be bought—
At any rate with money nowadays ;
No one would dare to entertain the thought
(Except perhaps a poet). Take the case
Of any single judge you like to name.
To be a judge at all he must have been
For years and years an adept at the game
Of advocacy, which I take to mean
The art of proving " two and two make five "
Or " black is white and white's a dirty grey ";
The art of sophists whereby villains thrive
And dismal innocents, who block the way
Of moneyed clients, learn to keep their place
Out of the road or underneath the wheels
That's art, that's advocacy, " that's my case ";
I've done it all, and I know how it feels.
It's pure enjoyment, it's a sport for kings,
And, unlike other sports, it pays its way
And pays it lavishly, until it brings
Promotion to the Bench on some proud day.

And then of course a miracle occurs,
Adam, K. C., is Mr Justice Adam,
No more obsequious to " Sir George " he purrs,
No more he dreams of briefs and fees, he's had 'em.
Sown in dishonour, he's to honour raised
And sees the front side of a " courtly bow " ;
Once briefed and bullied, flattered now and praised,
Corruption puts on incorruption now.
No longer now " for sale ", the dirty work
All left behind, he has so far out-soared
The shadow of that night that he would burke
All indiscreet allusions. He's " My Lord ! "
(O save the mark ! " My Lord ! " that little globe
Of sinful continence, that leering knave,
That pitiable prostitute ! What robe,
What ample wig can manumit the slave
Of purchased roguery ?) I beg your pardon,
We devils are constrained sometimes you know
To speak the truth ; but here in this my garden,
These pleasant courts, it is not often so.

" But does the right side never win ? " you ask.
Unfortunately yes, sometimes it does,
But only accidentally. The task

Confided to Beelzebub, my coz,
And to myself, is to suppress the truth,
And as the judges are in our possession
(All except two or three who in their youth
Somehow fell victims to the mad obsession
Of Christian principles) we find the work
Quite simple and straightforward. So you see
Why your St George afflicts me like a Turk,
And why *Sir* George is more the man for me.
" Plain Right can trust the jury ", do you say ?
We don't have juries here, my simple friend.
In Chancery you have the right to pay,
And that's where all your " rights " begin and end.
Vices are virtues here and fair is foul,
" No sentiment " 's the motto of our boast,
Pay for your " justice ", or be poor and howl ;
Hard hearts, hard cash, hard swearing rule the roast.

" But what about the dragon ? " do you ask.
Why dragon, snake or serpent, all is one,
Our serpent here puts on Sir George's mask,
And Eve is very speedily undone.
Still nose-led by the serpent, the poor wench
Remembers the old briefs and the fat fee

He used to pay, and still upon the Bench
She cries ' " Sir George for merry Germany ! "

Enter chorus of demons, who dance round and sing the
following ditty :

*When litigants throng to " the courts,"
And Dick, the counsel's clerk, exults,
When editors " condense" reports
And thus contrive, with faked results,
To " boost" their friends and kick their foes,
Unto the mill the good grist goes.*

*(Ding-Dong, ding dong, a merry peal,
While German George doth grease the wheel.)*

*When Englishmen pay German Jews
To prosecute their " son*-in-laws,"
When advocates their skill abuse
To make the worse the better cause ;
While honest people murmur " fudge,"
Then " sternly" speaks " the learned judge."* †

*(Ding-dong, ding-dong, a merry peal,
While German George doth grease the wheel.)*

The Devil and attendant demons vanish in a cloud of red smoke.
The Law Courts, however, remain.

1917.

---

* Or daughter.   *Vide* reports of recent cases.

† *Vide* the halfpenny press, *passim*, for the " judge's stern rebuke " so dear to the halfpenny sub-editorial heart.

THE DEVIL'S CARNIVAL

The Devil's Carnival

Shame like a pall shrouds this degenerate land
Where armoured honour once was wont to stand,
And the mocked sceptre slips from the weak hand.

Greed, Lust, vain Pride, and open Treachery
Cluster about the Throne. Behold and see
Asquith and Churchill, Smith and Bottomley,

Jew-bolstered Balfour, turn-coat Chamberlain,
" Converted " Curzon, and the lesser train
That hug with joy the Welsh attorney's chain.

Tried connoisseurs of his " refreshing fruits",
Each with the other valiantly disputes
Who most may lick his stercoraceous boots.

While round them in a ring the hireling Press
Obsequiously conspires to praise and bless
The leading welterers in the black mess;

Save where Commercial Patriotism's boast,
The Robert-Ross-admiring " *Morning Post* ",
With stolen thunder, or the re-hashed ghost

Of twelve-months-old " *Plain English* " makes it clear
How well George Lewis pulls strings in the rear,
While Miggs-like Bathurst still contrives to steer

Her shining course, designed not to be making
Trouble with Jews whose adverse shekel-raking
Might jeopardise a " business undertaking ".

And bold Northumberland ties up his purse,
And makes his one speech (prompted by his nurse)
While calling on the public to disburse.

Meanwhile the " Die-hards ", spoiling for a fight
(So they declare) continue to invite
" Subscriptions for the Cause ", while sitting tight

On their own money bags.   My country sweet,
These be thy " patriot " gods, while " Britons " bleat
Led by the super-Jew of Bolton Street

" *Plain English* " and hard hitting are no more,
And while the wily Hebrews grin or roar
The patriotic Muse becomes a whore.

The men who took the risks and gave the rubs
Are pushed aside by brainless dolts and cubs
And Conchie lands the cause in Wormwood Scrubbs.

Great God in heaven, is this the " sceptred isle "
That Shakespeare sang, is this the land whose smile
Was honour's prize, whose frown abashed the vile ?

One man there was enriching a high place
Who dared to beard dishonour to the face
And held no truck with salaried disgrace.

And he lies murdered now.   Murdered by whom ?
Whose will, conceived in what infernal womb
Of bloody thought, consigned him to his doom ?

Look you, to whom the profit? Whose the dread
Of Wilson living? Whose uneasy bed
Makes softer sleeping now that Wilson's dead?

Who fawned on Collins like a mongrel cur?
Who handed Ireland to a murderer?
Who gave His Feebleness dishonour's slur?

We see the shaft, but darkness hides the bow.
Who nursed the spirit that impelled the blow
That laid the Welshman's adversary low?

God knows, we guess, to what void soul it came
Reeking of hell, co-habitant with shame
Judas-companioned from th' eternal flame.

London, 26 June 1922.

TO ANOTHER JUDGE

To Another Judge

Blackness descends on England like a pall,
And in this obscene night, borne down and stoned,
Calling on God, lies Virtue. Brazen-toned
Through the shamed land rings out this trumpet call :
" Injustice shall be done though Heaven should fall. "
In the high places lo ! they sit enthroned,
Lust unashamed and Filthiness condoned
And crowned and comforted. Thou whited wall !

God shall smite thee. And for a present sign
I build this monument of lasting brass
Which shall enshrine thee till the world's last day.
We lately heard thy " judgment ". Mark now mine :
For ever be thou written down an ass
And down the ages bray and bray and bray !